THE UNCOMMON MINISTER

Winning Principles For Achieving Greatness In Your Ministry

VOLUME 3

MIKE MURDOCK

TABLE OF CONTENTS

Unless otherwise indicated, all Scripture quotations are taken from the King James Version of the Bible.

The Uncommon Minister, Volume 3
Copyright © 1999 by Mike Murdock
ISBN 1-56394-102-3

Published by The Wisdom Center
P. O. Box 99 • Denton, Texas 76202

To avoid the burdensome verbage of him/her; his, hers throughout this book, the simple reference to all of mankind, male or female, is simply "he" or "him."

∞ 1 ∞

MAKE SURE THE VOICE OF GOD IS THE FIRST VOICE YOU HEAR EVERY MORNING.

His voice is the only voice that truly matters.

Your people are wonderful. They lean on you. They depend on you. But your words will not bless and strengthen them *unless you have heard from God yourself.* You will not have the patience *and* endurance to handle their crisis unless you hear the voice of God yourself.

Your people cannot *talk* to God for you.

Your people cannot *know* the voice of God for you.

The psalmist discovered this, "O God, Thou art my God; early will I seek Thee: my soul thirsteth for Thee, my flesh longeth for Thee in a dry and thirsty land, where no water is; To see Thy power and Thy glory, so as I have seen Thee in the sanctuary" (Psalm 63:1,2).

What You Hear First Determines What You Speak Next.

One of the ingredients of The Perfect Day includes hearing the voice of God each morning.

You must hear His voice *before you hear the bad news about the economy*. He has promised supernatural provision. "Thou wilt keep him in perfect peace, whose mind is stayed on Thee: because he trusteth in Thee" (Isaiah 26:3).

You must hear His voice *before the report of the doctor comes*. God is your great physician. "Great peace have they which love Thy law: and nothing shall offend them" (Psalm 119:165).

You must hear His voice *before others have had an opportunity to influence you*. He alone knows the truth.

After you hear the voice of God, *the critical words of others have little affect upon you*. His presence reassures you. His words correct your course. His peace settles the storms within you.

After you hear His words, the *flattering words of others cannot puff you up*. Both feet are on the ground. Your instructions are clear.

After you hear The Voice of God, *you will not require the praise of others*. His confidence in you satisfies completely.

After you hear the voice of God, *your attitude will change instantly*. You will not face the future with anger, torment, or fear. He has spoken. His Words have settled every issue. Time will prove Him correct.

That's why listening to cassettes of the Scriptures are so important. *Every morning.* Without fail. Keep them in your car. Keep them beside your bed. Keep them in your office. Encourage your entire family to absorb the Word of God *daily* by cassette. Nothing you could give another could surpass the Bible on cassette tape. His Words are forever settled in heaven.

When you awaken, everything else often seems so urgent. Each phone call appears desperate. Every letter on your desk screams for attention. Everybody has a deserving request.

You will never create order until you make His presence your priority.

10 Reasons You Should Hear The Voice Of God First

1. *Hear His Voice Before You Return Any Phone Calls To Those In Trouble.* Why? You will not know how to respond properly until you have The Mentor's manna. Each day will require a fresh anointing for the different needs of your ministry.

2. *Hear His Voice Before You Answer Any Letters.* Why? You may make wrong commitments and promises you cannot fulfill. Respond to His *commands* instead of the *needs* of people.

3. *Hear His Voice Before You Listen To The Voices Of Others.* Why? Their *problems* are driving them, while the *plan of God* should be wooing you. Others are driven by their needs. You must be *led* by the commands of God.

4. *Hear His Voice Before You Listen To The Complaints Of Others.* Why? His peace will keep you. He can calm your spirit and rest your mind. You are not responsible for the happiness of others. That is a work of the Spirit.

5. *Hear His Voice Before You Embrace The Ideas Of Others.* Why? The ideas of men are not the

commands of God. The doubts and fears of people are like magnets. They attach themselves to your spirit dragging you down like the barnacles on a ship. You become emotionally paralyzed by carrying around their baggage.

6. *Hear His Voice Before Responding To Any Requests Of Others.* Why? You must *qualify the soil* before you give to someone. Your Seed is precious. The Seed of your Time, Love or Money deserves a *screening process.* Don't sow everything into everyone. *Qualify the soil.* Stony ground? Thorny ground? It is so easy to be persuaded by people. Wrong people. Oh, how I wish I could go back and change some of the Seed sowing that I have done. I allowed the faces of people to affect my Seed sowing. Some have cried "crocodile tears." I was affected. On more than one occasion, I have emptied my pockets to someone who was actually unqualified to receive. Why? I had not been in His presence to hear His voice. *Good Seed deserves good soil.*

7. *Hear His Voice Before Revealing Your Dreams Or Discoveries To Others.* Why? When the wrong people hear your dreams, they can sabotage your faith for them. When Satan Wants To Destroy You, He Puts A Person Close To You. A wrong person. Wrong people sow Seeds of doubt and unbelief.

8. *Hear His Voice Before You Pursue The Approval Of Others.* Why? Pride can destroy you. Praise feeds pride. "These six things doth the Lord hate: yea, seven are an abomination unto him: A proud look, a lying tongue. An heart that deviseth wicked imaginations, feet that be swift in running to mischief, A false witness that speaketh lies, and

he that soweth discord among brethren" (Proverbs 6:16-19).

Praise is often excessive, cunning and deceptive. It is often used to manipulate ministers into an intimate relationship or an unwise decision. Flattery is satanic. Hearing His voice *protects you* from these arrows that fly relentlessly toward your life.

9. *Hear His Voice Before Absorbing Disturbing News Reports.* "I rejoice at Thy Word, as one that findeth great spoil" (Psalm 119:162).

"Great peace have they which love Thy law: and nothing shall offend them" (Psalm 119:165).

"Thou wilt keep him in perfect peace, whose mind is stayed on Thee: because he trusteth in Thee" (Isaiah 26:3).

10. *Hear His Voice Before Making Significant Changes In Your Ministry.*

You were never given the responsibility of planning your ministry.

You were given the responsibility of *discovering His plan* for your ministry.

Make Sure The Voice Of God Is The First Voice You Hear Every Morning.

It is One of the Secrets of the Uncommon Minister.

∾ 2 ∾

GIVE AN ALTAR CALL IN EVERY SERVICE.

An altar call is a door to change.

An altar call is your personal invitation to others to respond specifically to the message you have just ministered.

When you preach *salvation*, you should *invite* those present to make a decision to follow Christ.

When you preach *healing*, you should *invite* those who want to experience healing to come forward and receive that miracle from God.

When you preach *commitment* to Christian service, you should *invite* those present to come forward and dedicate their lives to be used of the Lord in His work.

Imagine a lawyer spending hours presenting a case in a court and then walking out without ever asking the jury for a verdict! Imagine a salesman talking about the automobile you are viewing for possible purchasing and walking away without ever asking you, "Can I write this contract up for you today?"

Preaching requires a decision.

Your altar call can be varied, presented creatively and at different times in a service. But it is important that you recognize the *necessity* of it.

In my early ministry, I remember the pastor coming up to conclude a service after I had ministered. He would simply ask, "How many people tonight need to accept Christ as your personal Savior?" As I sat there embarrassed and humiliated, I watched many come to Christ under the pastor's personal invitation, because I was too focused on my teaching rather than their decision about it.

10 Important Keys Every Minister Should Know About Altar Calls

1. *Make Your Altar Call Easy To Understand.* I remember being in a huge church in California where the pastor gave detailed instructions. "Pick up your purse and your Bible and make certain all your belongings are in your hand. Now, come to the front and place your feet against this platform." He was almost ridiculous in the details. But over the years I discovered how important it was that the people coming would know exactly *why* they were coming, and *what would occur.* Explain how long you will require them to stand at the front or meet with counselors in a private room.

2. *Give Enough Information To Remove Any Fears, Discomfort, Or Uncertainty About The Altar Call.* Recently, a pastor had visitors come forward and follow a man into a room in the back of the church for private counseling. I sat there shocked. You see, he told them to follow a man they had never seen in their life to a strange room that was uncomfortable and foreign to them for advice they never really asked for. As a visitor, I would have never followed that instruction. I would have sat

down and gone back home and talked to God in my private time. It is important that you remove any potential discomfort for those responding to an altar call. (That's why I present my own altar call in a very different fashion and at the *beginning* of any service instead of the end.)

3. *Give An Altar Call Anywhere And Any Time The Holy Spirits Leads You.* R. A. Torrey, the great preacher of many years ago, had a tragic and unforgettable experience. As he sat in a restaurant with friends, the Holy Spirit impressed him to talk to the waiter about his soul. The countenance of the waiter had stirred him. But in an effort to keep a relaxed atmosphere, he ignored the prompting of the Holy Spirit. Approximately one and a half hours later he noticed that the waiter had never returned to his table. He inquired about the waiter. The manager replied that they had just found the young man in the back of the restaurant, *hanging*. He had committed suicide during the meal. R. A. Torrey used this to encourage young ministers to always follow the leadership of the Holy Spirit in leading someone to Christ.

4. *Keep Your Altar Calls Simple, Avoiding Doctrinal Controversy.* There's a time for doctrinal teaching. The altar call is a time for a simple decision about experiencing God or the supernatural miracle He has promised.

5. *Appeal To The Heart, Not The Intellect, During Your Altar Call.* Explain what you are talking about in terms others can understand. Some do not understand the phrase, "Born again." Recognize that the jargon and vocabulary of every church group varies.

6. *Never Assume Everyone Present Really Understands The Gospel.* They do not. That Which Becomes Familiar Often Becomes Hidden From Us. We are so familiar with the gospel that we assume everyone understands it fully.

7. *Never Schedule Too Many Things In A Service To Overlook The Most Important Thing— Accepting Jesus As Your Personal Savior.* Remember that a short altar call can often be just as effective as a long altar call. Some of my most effective altar calls have taken less than three minutes to give. The Holy Spirit was already working. I simply needed to "pull in the net."

8. *Allow The Holy Spirit Enough Time To Speak To People.* Don't rush every altar call. Great decisions sometimes require extra time. I have watched uncommon evangelists linger long during an altar call so that "just one more can come to Christ." Some of the greatest conversions on earth have taken place in the last few seconds of a lingering altar call.

9. *Listen Continuously For The Timing Of The Holy Spirit Regarding Your Altar Call.* God uses me in the first few minutes of a service to present an altar call. In the ministries of others, He moves differently. *Find the pattern* God provides for your own ministry and in specific services, and you will see the hand of God move miraculously in every service.

10. *Expect The Holy Spirit To Do His Work In The Hearts Of Others.* You are not the human persuader. The *Holy Spirit* persuades. You are the *presenter* of the gospel, *not* the persuader of the message. Your message, or altar call, should present

the facts necessary for a decision to be made. You must trust the Holy Spirit to do His work, in His timing, in the hearts of the people.

Give An Altar Call In Every Service You Minister.

It is One of the Secrets of The Uncommon Minister.

❦ 3 ❦

STOP EXPECTING EVERYONE TO UNDERSTAND YOUR STYLE OF MINISTRY.

Your friends celebrate your difference.
Your enemies *despise* your difference.
Your congregation has responded to your *difference*, not your similarity to other ministries.

God has made you unlike other ministers for a reason. The Apostle Paul reached those that Peter could not reach. Jeremiah reached those that Jonah could not reach. Jesus chose 12 disciples, not one.

God holds you accountable for finding your difference from other ministries. "Now there are diversities of gifts, but the same Spirit. And there are differences of administrations, but the same Lord. And there are diversities of operations, but it is the same God which worketh all in all" (1 Corinthians 12:4-6).

Uncommon Ministers know that many will not respond to them and accept their ministry. One of the most effective teachers in Christianity is Dr. Frederick K. C. Price. On page 39 in his book, "Practical Suggestions for Successful Ministry," he writes, *"Only certain people listen to me.* There are people who would not cross the street to hear me. And I know this! I do not operate under any illusions.

Everyone does not like my *method* of teaching; everyone is not *ready* for me; and I'm not ready for everybody. I know it and I don't sweat it. I am believing God is going to send the people to me who will respond to my kind of *personality*, my kind of *ministry*, my kind of whatever it might be."

Some ministers have a universal appeal to keep the masses of humanity aware of God and the Bible. Billy Graham has such a ministry. Nothing in his message has been extreme. His Assignment is connected to the masses.

Some ministers are raised up to solve a specific problem for a group of people. Healing ministries are raised up for the sick. Some ministries have one focus—feeding children who are hungry. Some ministries are obsessed with freeing drug addicts from cocaine. You are assigned to somebody, not *everyone*.

Those who do not discern your difference and gift become unqualified for a relationship with you. Do everything you can to explain your ministry effectively, thoroughly and repetitiously enough to be understood. When it is refused, "keep fishing" for those who want the message God has given you.

Major ministries will write a new friend or partner for a few weeks. Then, they suddenly stop. Why? They realize that the several letters invested were not understood, appreciated or desired by the new friend. So, they keep reaching to others who *do* want what they have.

You are not assigned to everybody.

Stop Expecting Everyone To Understand Your Style Of Ministry.

It is One of the Secrets of The Uncommon Minister.

≈ 4 ≈

NEGOTIATE EVERYTHING.

Nothing is ever as it first appears.
I walked into a luggage store here in Dallas many years ago. When I had selected the luggage I desired, I asked the young lady if she could provide a *"corporate discount."*

"What is a corporate discount?"

"Forty percent off."

"All right!" was her reply.

With one simple question, I saved several hundred dollars. *Negotiate everything.*

While standing at the airline counter, I was informed that my excess baggage was over $200.

"I was hoping you would show me a little mercy today," I joked gently.

The agent thought for a few moments and replied, "All right." With one simple statement, I saved over $200.

▶ *Your words are making you more money or costing you.*

▶ *Your words are bringing Increase or Decrease.*

▶ *Your words are creating Doors or Walls.*

▶ *Your words are Bridges or Barricades.*

The Scriptures teach it: "A man shall eat good by the fruit of his mouth" (Proverbs 13:2). "The wicked is snared by the transgression of his lips: but the just shall come out of trouble" (Proverbs 12:13).

7 Facts You Should Remember When Negotiating With Others

1. *Successful Negotiation Requires The Right Attitude.* Nobody wants to be taken lightly, intimidated or pushed. Everybody is involved. The lady in the luggage store wanted to sell the luggage, create favor and a happy customer. *I gave her the information that would accommodate that need—* forty percent discount. I returned later to buy many other items because of the favor she showed.

The airline that gave me the excess baggage for free has since received over $100,000 of my transportation business. Negotiation should be a win-win situation for everybody involved.

2. *Successful Negotiation Requires An Understanding Of The Cost Involved For Others.* Donald Trump explained why his father was so successful in negotiating prices. His father invested time in finding out *exactly what the cost was* for those he was negotiating with... so he would know exactly how far to negotiate.

3. *Successful Negotiation Requires Proper Timing.* Many years ago, I was very weary when I arrived home from a meeting. The flight was tiresome. As I walked into the office, a staff member approached me.

"I've got to talk to you!"

"All right. Sit down. How can I help you?"

She was very aggressive and flippant. "I need a raise!"

"Well, how much are you wanting me to increase

your salary each month?" I asked.

"I need $1,000 a month raise."

I really thought she was joking. She wasn't. She continued, "My husband and I are moving into a new home that we have just built, and I really need the income to pay for the house."

It was so ridiculous to me, I almost laughed aloud. I advised her gently that I understood her need. Perhaps, it would be well for her to find another job where she could secure the salary she needed.

"Your present salary was created by a list of problems you chose to solve for me. Now, you want a huge increase in salary. Do you have a list of the *new* problems you will begin to solve for me?" I asked

It never crossed her mind to solve more problems for her more salary.

4. *Successful Negotiation Involves Long-Term Gain, Not Short-Term Gain.* The famous billionaire, Sam Walton, said he never invested in a company for where it would be in 18 months. He invested in companies that would succeed ten years down the road. Employees can often squeeze out an extra dollar from a boss during a crisis situation. But, if it causes a wall of separation, that staff person often causes himself a deeper problem in the long term.

5. *Successful Negotiation Should Focus On Details That Truly Matter.* Several years ago, a wonderful young couple wrote me about a job. They were making $5.00 an hour. He was riding a motorcycle to a second job. He had three children and worked sixteen hours a day on two jobs at $10.00

an hour total. They were destitute. My heart went out to them. They had driven all night to meet me face-to-face for an interview. I agreed to pay him what *both* of his jobs were presently providing for working 16 hours a day. As a gesture of caring, I provided a home free for some extra yard work. They were thrilled and elated. Over a period of time, I also provided furniture, dishes, clothes, and even a car. They were enjoyable, so I was happy to do so.

Eventually, someone influenced them to negotiate for more, at every opportunity to "squeeze me." Every time something broke, they "squeezed me." I noticed a pattern. It became one-sided.

When you have many employees in your ministry, you cannot give everyone a raise when you desire to do so. You can't always give it to them the moment they deserve it. You have to think long term for the ministry. Something within me became agitated. So, when the oven broke down, they wanted me to replace it. I was weary of replacing everything. I requested that they pay half, and I would pay the other half. They attempted to use harsh words to negotiate with me. I'm not the kind to respond favorably to intimidation of any sort.

I realized they were frustrated. So, I explained that they had 45 days to go find a new house, and they could purchase it themselves. Yes, they were good people, but poor negotiators. They lost a wonderful blessing trying to squeeze me for "an extra nickel." *Don't lose dollars* trying to save pennies.

▶ *Close doors gently.* If you realize that you have to end a relationship, close doors quietly. You may have to return through them again in the coming years.

▶ *Never burn bridges behind you.* Everybody talks. Everything you do is being discussed by those that you have not yet met. Don't schedule unnecessary conflicts in your future.

6. *Attend Negotiation Seminars, Listen To Tapes, And Secure The Counsel Of Qualified Mentors Before Doing Any Serious Negotiation.*

7. *Successful Negotiation Requires Quality Time.* Don't rush anything. Run from the salesman who insists that "this is the last day of this sale." Don't fall for it. When you return a month later, they will still deal! They need your purchase more than they need their own product. Your opinion deserves to be heard. Just make certain that it is heard at the right *time* in the right *atmosphere...* with the right *attitude.*

Negotiate Everything.

It is One of the Secrets of The Uncommon Minister.

≈ 5 ≈

NEVER ASSUME YOUR INSTRUCTIONS ARE BEING UNDERSTOOD AND COMPLETED.

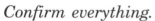

Confirm everything.

I have marveled that so many have kept their jobs over the years. Few seem to *follow through* on instructions given to them by their supervisors.

True, there are a few close to you who may have proven themselves over a long period of time. They understand you. They are diligent, aggressive and trustworthy. My own experience is that there will be *less than three people* in your life that you can consistently count on to complete your instructions without your personal supervision or follow-up.

4 Clues That Your Instruction Will Probably Not Be Followed

1. *When They Do Not Regularly Carry Paper And Pen.* Never count on any person who does not regularly carry paper and pen in their hand to follow through on something you've asked them to do. *Never.* The unlearned trust their memory for

everything.

2. *When They Fail To Reach For Paper And Pen To Document The Instruction The Very Moment You Give It To Them.* Some carry paper and pen, but simply nod when you give them instruction. They do not *write* it down. They do not *document* it. They trust their memory. The instruction will be *forgotten* in their busyness and overconfidence. Bank on it.

3. *When They Ask No Additional Questions About The Assignment Or Instruction.* That's another clue. Few instructions are complete at the beginning. When you ask them to telephone someone about an item, they *should* ask:

    a. Is there a *deadline* on this?

    b. When do you need a *report back* on the results of this telephone call?

    c. Is there anything *additional* I should know?

When additional questions are never asked following an instruction received, *they're not giving any thought to it.*

4. *When They Make A Statement, "I will really try to get to that, sir." They won't get to it.* The word "*try*" reveals half-heartedness.

5 Helpful Keys In Giving Instructions To Your Staff

1. *Give The Instruction To One Person Only.* When two receive it, they usually expect the other to do it.

2. *Document The Date You Gave The Instruction To Them.*

3. *Require A Specific Status Report On A*

Specific Date. This shows you the progress and the expected date of completion.

    4.   *Clearly Explain The Urgency Of The Instruction And Its Importance.*

    5.   *Never Give An Instruction To Someone Unqualified To Complete It.*

    Never Assume Your Instructions Are Being Understood And Completed.

    It is One of the Secrets of The Uncommon Minister.

≈ 6 ≈

KEEP A BOOK WITH YOU AT ALL TIMES.

―――>಄€―――

Make moments count.
What you read is what you will become.
Reading prevents boredom. That's why magazines
and books are kept in the waiting rooms of physicians
and hospitals. When you bring the book of your
choice with you, you can maintain a continuous flow
of appropriate information into your heart and mind.

6 Facts Every Minister Should Remember About Reading

1. *Reading Will Often Discourage Unpro-
ductive Conversation With Others.* Have you ever
sat besides someone who could not stop talking?
Unfortunately, most people who love to talk a lot do
not require anything significant to energize them.
They will talk about anything just to avoid silence.
When you keep a book handy, this usually
discourages them.

2. *Keep A List Of The Books You Want To
Read Each Month.* This prevents unwise selections
in moments of boredom or fatigue. Every minister
should read at least one book a week. At the
beginning of each year, select 52 books that you would

like to complete by the end of the year and select a new one each Sunday. Just 20 pages a day will take you through a 140 page book every week.

3. *Bring Books With You On Airplane Trips And Vacations.* You are away from the busyness of your daily schedule. The phone cannot ring. The television is off. You can withdraw in your own private mental world. Focus is possible. You can purchase books in airports, but it is better for you to bring your own choice with you.

4. *Keep Reading Material In Your Washroom.* Avoid two year old magazines that do not keep you current and energized. Place books there that are priority and important to you. I keep a Bible with my books as well.

5. *Keep Two Books In Your Automobile At All Times.* I suggest keeping a fiction book and a non-fiction book simultaneously. Moods vary. Sometimes, you want to *relax* and other times you will want to *learn*. Keep *both* convenient for such occasions. During traffic jams, this relieves the stress of "doing nothing" en route to an appointment.

6. *Make Books Accessible To Others Riding With You As Well.* This reading habit "brings your thoughts into captivity." This neutralizes the influence of others around you who would use these occasions to break your focus. *Your life stays on course.* Your focus is *protected*. You continue to grow even in the spare moments between appointments.

My life is quite full. There is little time for loneliness, self pity or "down time." *Every moment matters to me.* My hours matter to me. I travel a lot. I have for 34 years. I have noticed that the only time I want to read a novel is for relaxation on a plane. When I am home, I am emotionally attached to my projects and feeling the responsibility of 31 staff members. So, I will take those moments on an airplane to nap (power naps), read the newspaper, or read a novel. Ten years ago, I would write letters on planes and review business proposals. That has changed as well.

Your needs continuously change. Familiarize yourself with your personal rhythms. Cooperate with them and you can become more productive than you really realize.

Do not fight against the surges of energy in your life and ministry. Identify and flow with them. Make moments count.

Keep A Book With You At All Times.

It is One of the Secrets of The Uncommon Minister.

～ 7 ～

STOP BELITTLING YOUR PEOPLE FOR THEIR PURSUIT OF PROSPERITY.

———————

Financial provision is a reward, not a curse.

God wants to bless His people. "No good thing will He withhold from them that walk uprightly" (Psalm 84:11).

I have heard some ministers publicly sneer at "prosperity preachers," and preach long messages on the snares of riches, while scores of their own people were desperate without jobs, impoverished and bankrupt. *Only fools lecture on drowning during a drought.*

Late one night, I sat in a pastor's car. He was agitated. I had taught at length that night about our God of supernatural provision, the blessings that God wanted us to experience in our life. I addressed becoming debt free, bringing the tithe to the Lord, and even putting your children through college. He had three basic fears.

3 Basic Fears Many Ministers Have About Receiving Offerings

1. *He Feared Criticism From The Wealthy Of His Congregation.*

MIKE MURDOCK ■ 27

2. *He Was Unpursuaded Concerning The Harvest That God Promised His People For Giving.*
3. *He Believed It Was Improper To Emphasize Finances In A Spiritual Atmosphere.*

As we talked, he slowly developed an understanding:

The wealthy are often unconcerned about the harvest of the poor. That's why Jesus declared, "The Spirit of the Lord is upon Me, because He that anointed Me to preach the gospel to the poor" (Luke 4:18).

The Lord of the harvest cannot lie. He will honor the Seeds of His people. "But this I say, He which soweth sparingly shall reap also sparingly; and he which soweth bountifully shall reap also bountifully" (2 Corinthians 9:6).

The church is the most appropriate place on earth for faith in God to be unlocked for finances. Why permit your people to pursue financial blessing in an environment of money hungry, greedy, God-hating, God-ignoring hypocrites of the world system? Why can't we come into His presence with great expectation that we will receive what we need from our Father's hand? (Read Matthew 6:33.)

I asked this minister five simple questions.

Five Questions I Wish Every Pastor Would Answer

1. "Do you have widows that cannot pay their apartment rent?" He did.
2. "Do you have people out of jobs?" He did.
3. "Have you made financial promises to missionaries that have been difficult to fulfill?" He had.

4. "Could you reach more souls with the gospel in this city if you had more money for television and radio ministry?" He replied that it was the dream of his heart to reach his city.

5. "Who have *you* chosen as the Financial Mentor of your people?" That shocked him. He had made no plans at all for any Financial Mentor or Deliverer to come to his church and educate his people on budgets, debt, and Seed faith.

Yes, it is true, occasionally you will meet someone with more money than they will ever need or use. For them, the message on prosperity may seem unneeded, unheeded and unnecessary. This kind of logic would cause you to stop to preaching salvation in the presence of believers!

Please, please, stop discouraging your people from believing, expecting, and receiving an Uncommon Provision from their Uncommon Provider.

▶ Their *future* depends on their *provision.*
▶ The future of your *church* depends on their *understanding* of sowing and reaping.
▶ The future of *souls* waiting to hear the gospel depends on *their support* of the gospel.

The Uncommon Minister will never discourage and weaken the desires of His people toward financial provision and prosperity.

Never Belittle Your People For Their Pursuit Of Prosperity.

It is One of the Secrets of The Uncommon Minister.

WISDOM KEYS FOR AN UNCOMMON MINISTRY.

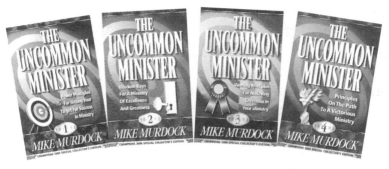

Complete your personal library of
"The Uncommon Minister" Series. These first seven
volumes are a must for your ministry reading.
Practical and powerful, these Wisdom Keys will
enhance your ministry expression for years to come.

ITEM	TITLE	QTY	PRICE	TOTAL
B107	The Uncommon Minister, Volume 1		$5.00	$
B108	The Uncommon Minister, Volume 2		$5.00	$
B109	The Uncommon Minister, Volume 3		$5.00	$
B110	The Uncommon Minister, Volume 4		$5.00	$
B111	The Uncommon Minister, Volume 5		$5.00	$
B112	The Uncommon Minister, Volume 6		$5.00	$
B113	The Uncommon Minister, Volume 7		$5.00	$
All 7 Volumes of The Uncommon Minister			$35.00	$

Mail To: **The Wisdom Center** P.O. Box 99 Denton, TX 76202 940-891-1400		
	Add 10% For Shipping	$
	(Canada add 20% to retail cost and 20% shipping)	$
	Enclosed Is My Seed-Faith Gift For Your Ministry	$
	Total Amount Enclosed	$

SORRY NO C.O.D.'S

Name _____
Address _____
City _____
State _____
Zip _____   Telephone _____

☐ Check   ☐ Money Order
☐ Visa   ☐ Master Card   ☐ Amex

Signature _____
Exp. Date _____
Card No. _____

THE
WISDOM
CENTER

———— **Quantity Prices for** ————
"The Uncommon Minister" Series

1-9	=	$5.00 each
10-99	=	$4.00 each (20% discount)
100-499	=	$3.50 each (30% discount)
500-999	=	$3.00 each (40% discount)
1,000-up	=	$2.50 each (50% discount)
5,000-up	=	$2.00 each (60% discount)

POWERFUL WISDOM BOOKS FROM DR. MIKE MURDOCK!

You can increase your Wisdom Library by purchasing any one of these great titles by *MIKE MURDOCK*. Scriptural, practical, readable. These books are life-changing!

The Covenant Of 58 Blessings

Dr. Murdock shares the phenomenon of the 58 Blessings, his experiences, testimonials, and the words of God Himself concerning the 58 Blessings. Your life will never be the same! (Paperback)
(B47) 86 pages $8

Wisdom - God's Golden Key To Success

In this book, *Dr. Mike Murdock* shares his insight into the Wisdom of God that will remove the veil of ignorance and propel you into the abundant life. (Paperback)
(B70) 67 pages $7

The Proverbs 31 Woman

God's ultimate woman is described in Proverbs 31. *Dr. Murdock* breaks it down to the pure revelation of these 31 marvelous qualities. (Paperback)
(B49) 68 pages $7

Secrets Of The Richest Man Who Ever Lived

This teaching on the life of Solomon will bring you to a higher level of understanding in the 31 secrets of uncommon wealth and success. God's best will soon be yours as you learn and put into practice these keys. (Paperback)
(B99) 192 pages $10

Remember...God sent His Son, but He left His Book!

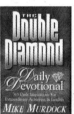

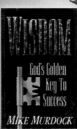

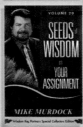

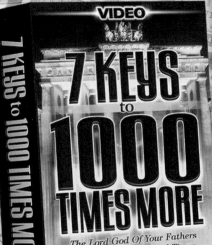

Somebody's Future Will Not Begin Until You Enter.

The Secret Place
Library Pak

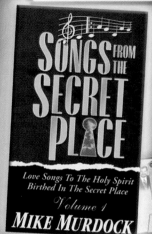

Songs from the Secret Place

Over 40 Great Songs On 6 Music Tapes
Including "I'm In Love" / Love Songs From The Holy Spirit
Birthed In The Secret Place / <u>Side A</u> Is Dr. Mike Murdock
Singing / <u>Side B</u> Is Music Only For Your Personal Prayer Time

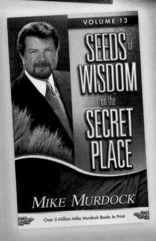

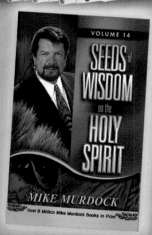

Seeds of Wisdom on the Secret Place

4 Secrets The Holy Spirit Reveals In The Secret Place / The Necessary
Ingredients In Creating Your Secret Place / 10 Miracles That Will
Happen In The Secret Place

Seeds of Wisdom on the Holy Spirit

The Protocol For Entering The Presence Of
The Holy Spirit / the greatest day of my life and
What Made It So / Power Keys For Developing Your
Personal Relationship With The Holy Spirit

Wisdom Is The Principal Thing
Book/Tape Pak
SP PAK-001 / $30
Six Audio Tapes & Two Books
(A $40 Value!)
The Wisdom Center

ORDER TODAY!
www.thewisdomcenter.cc

1-888-WISDOM-1
(1-888-947-3661)

THE WISDOM CENTER • P.O. Box 99 • Denton, Texas 76202

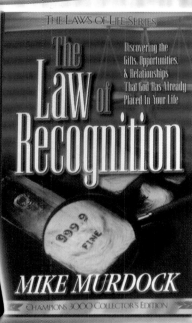

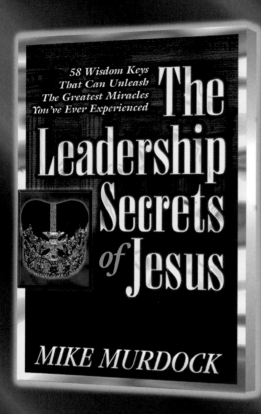

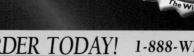

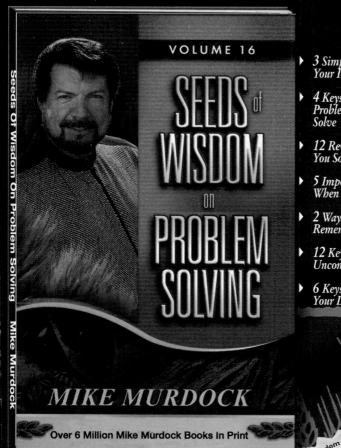

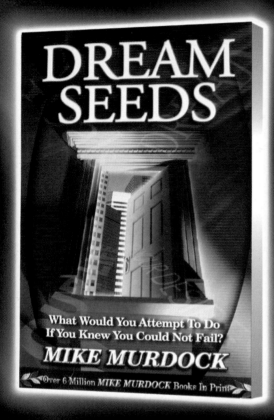

Where You Are Determines What Grows In You.

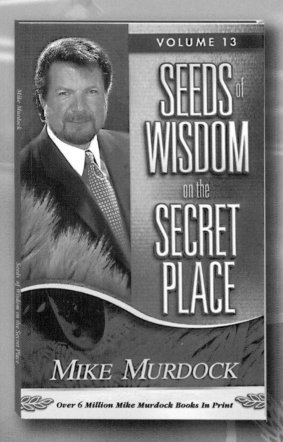

VOLUME 13

SEEDS of WISDOM on the SECRET PLACE

MIKE MURDOCK

Over 6 Million Mike Murdock Books In Print

▶ 4 Secrets The Holy Spirit Reveals In The Secret Place

▶ Master Keys in Cultivating An Effective Prayer Life

▶ The Necessary Ingredients In Creating Your Secret Place

▶ 10 Miracles That Will Happen In The Secret Place

Wisdom Is The Principal Thing

Book B-115 / $5

The Wisdom Center

Run To Win.

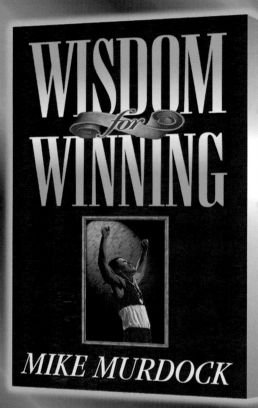

- ▸ 10 Ingredients For Success
- ▸ Ten Lies Many People Believe About Money
- ▸ 20 Keys For Winning At Work
- ▸ 20 Keys To A Better Marriage
- ▸ 3 Facts Every Parent Should Remember
- ▸ 5 Steps Out Of Depression
- ▸ The Greatest Wisdom Principle I Ever Learned
- ▸ 7 Keys To Answered Prayer
- ▸ God's Master Golden Key To Total Success
- ▸ The Key To Understanding Life

Everyone needs to feel they have achieved something with their life. When we stop producing, loneliness and laziness will choke all enthusiasm from our living. What would you like to be doing? What are you doing about it? Get started on a project in your life. Start building on your dreams. Resist those who would control and change your personal goals. Get going with this powerful teaching and reach your life goals!

Wisdom Is The Principal Thing
Book B-01 / $10
Six Audio Tapes TS-01 / $30
The Wisdom Center

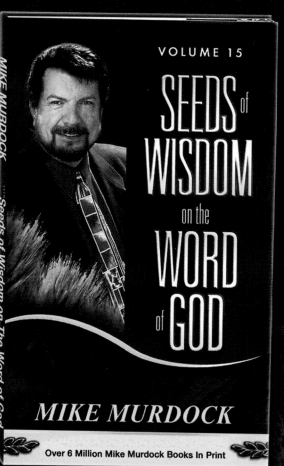

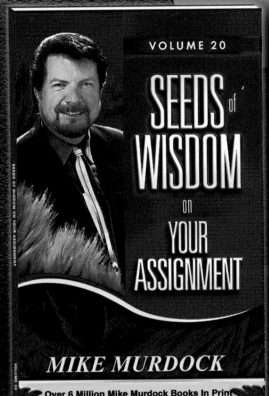

WISDOM COLLECTION

8

SECRETS OF THE UNCOMMON MILLIONAIRE

1. The Uncommon Millionaire Conference Vol. 1 (Six Cassettes)
2. The Uncommon Millionaire Conference Vol. 2 (Six Cassettes)
3. The Uncommon Millionaire Conference Vol. 3 (Six Cassettes)
4. The Uncommon Millionaire Conference Vol. 4 (Six Cassettes)
5. 31 Reasons People Do Not Receive Their Financial Harvest (256 Page Book)
6. Secrets of the Richest Man Who Ever Lived (178 Page Book)
7. 12 Seeds of Wisdom Books On 12 Topics
8. The Gift of Wisdom for Leaders Desk Calendar
9. Songs From The Secret Place (Music Cassette)
10. In Honor of the Holy Spirit (Music Cassette)
11. 365 Memorization Scriptures On The Word Of God (Audio Cassette)